Locomotives and Recollections
No 6233 DUCHESS OF SUTHERLAND

John Whitehouse

© John Whitehouse 2021

All rights reserved. No part of this publication may be reproduced, stored in a retrieval system or transmitted, in any form or by any means, electronic, mechanical, photocopying, recording or otherwise, without prior permission in writing from Silver Link Books, Mortons Media Group Ltd.

First published in 2021

British Library Cataloguing in Publication Data

A catalogue record for this book is available from the British Library.

ISBN 978 1 85794 589 8

Silver Link Books
Mortons Media Group Limited
Media Centre
Morton Way
Horncastle
LN9 6JR
Tel/Fax: 01507 529535

email: sohara@mortons.co.uk
Website: www.nostalgiacollection.com

Printed and bound in the Czech Republic

Title page: Duchess of Sutherland is positioned outside the Princess Royal Class Locomotive Trust's West Shed on 9 September 2018, immaculate in the recently applied LMS 'Midland Red' livery. This was the livery carried when the locomotive first returned to traffic in 2001. *JW*

Contents

Introduction	3
LMS and British Railways	7
Into preservation: from Crewe to Butlin's and Bressingham	10
The West Shed	13
The West Coast Main Line	15
The Settle & Carlisle line	25
The North West	31
The North Wales Coast Line	35
The Welsh Borders	39
The Midlands	40
The South Midlands	46
Overhaul	48
Scotland	49
The Royal Train	54
Heritage lines	57
The East Coast Main Line and connections	59
The Midland Main Line	67
South and South West England	75
Index of locations	Inside back cover

Bibliography

Usually with such projects multiple sources of reference are normal, but in this case there needed to be just one: *6233 Duchess of Sutherland and The Princess Coronation Class* by Brell Ewart and Brian Radford, published in November 2002 by the Princess Royal Class Locomotive Trust (ISBN 0-9543969-0-1). It is a fascinating book, full of comprehensive detail not only covering the history of *Duchess of Sutherland* up to the date of publication, but also of the 'Princess Coronation' Class in general. It is highly recommended.

Dedication

'In loving memory of my Dad and the times we spent on the bridge at Milford, hoping the next one would be a 'Duchess'.

Acknowledgements

Compiling a volume such as this is always going to be more complicated than anticipated, and I am truly grateful to all the people who have, without exception, responded magnificently to my pleadings for help. First, my grateful thanks to all the photographers who made their work available and whose contribution has greatly enhanced the scope of this book. Their photographs are individually credited as part of the respective caption. Particular mention, though, goes to David Cross, who kindly made available images taken by his late father, the renowned railway photographer Derek Cross. A special mention, too, for Malcolm Baker and Paul Wood, both trustees of the Princess Royal Class Locomotive Trust, who over the years have provided a wealth of information and anecdotes concerning the operations of *Duchess of Sutherland*. Once again Richard Tuplin has taken on the task of proofreading and making sense of my ramblings. For that I am truly grateful, and am pleased to hear that he is likely to make a full recovery from this ordeal.

Introduction

Family folklore says that my grandfather took me to 'see the trains' when I must have been little more than three years old. The chosen spot was the road bridge that spanned the Trent Valley Line at the site of the now long-closed Milford & Brocton station. Although I remember little from that time, there is no doubt that an appreciation of the majesty of a 'Duchess', emerging from the portal of Shugborough Tunnel at speed, became hard-wired into my psyche. To reinforce that induction, my first 'train-set', Hornby-Dublo of course, came with No 46232 *Duchess of Montrose*, and my affection for the class was complete!

In later life, when a renewed interest in railways took hold, the chance to see a 'Duchess' again in traffic became a dream, which I did not expect, at the time, to be fulfilled. Happily, I can now reflect back on more than four decades of enjoying the sight of a 'Duchess' once more on the main line. First to return was No 46229 *Duchess of Hamilton* followed by the subject of this book, No 46233 *Duchess of Sutherland*. Additionally, there is still the chance to visit the third preserved member of the class, No 46235 *City of Birmingham*, on static display at the Birmingham 'Think Tank'.

Duchess of Sutherland returned to main-line duties in 2001, since which time I have had the great pleasure of following her around the country with my camera. During that time, the 'Duchess' has visited many places not normally associated with the class, and this book is intended to provide a pictorial record of many of those journeys. It is not a history of *Duchess of Sutherland*, but a reflection of her life and times back on the main line, together with visits to heritage lines.

However, to put the story of *Duchess of Sutherland* into context, a brief historical overview is needed. For instance, why did the London Midland & Scottish Railway (LMS) have such a need for these locomotives in the first place? Between the wars an intense rivalry had developed between the LMS and the London & North Eastern Railway (LNER) for dominance on the prime London to Scotland axis, especially after the LNER introduced its new 'A4' Class streamlined locomotives in 1935.

The LMS needed something special in response to the 'A4s', and it came courtesy of the company's new Chief Mechanical Engineer, William A. Stanier (later Sir William). Trained by the Great Western Railway at Swindon Works, and working alongside Thomas Coleman, Chief Draughtsman at Derby, William Stanier developed a new locomotive that was designed to have not only the power, but also the grace, to take on the opposition. Compared to the LMS West Coast Main Line, the rival LNER's East Coast route was a billiard table, while

LLANFAIRFECHAN With the sun glinting off the Irish Sea, *Duchess of Sutherland* heads the empty coaching stock (ECS) of the Royal Train from Holyhead to Llandudno Junction. *JW*

the LMS had to operate heavy express trains over the fearsome northern fells. Therefore the new locomotives had to be able to haul such express trains and the heavier sleeper services over the steep gradients of Grayrigg, Shap and Beattock unassisted, while also having a turn of speed to match the competition.

These new locomotives were the 'Princess Coronation' Class, affectionately known as 'Duchesses', and were a further development and improvement of the earlier 'Princess Royal' Class. In response to the 'A4s', the first batch of five locomotives were streamlined and entered traffic in 1937, primarily to work the new 'Coronation' high-speed service between London Euston and Glasgow Central.

A further ten locomotives were ordered for delivery in 1938, of which just five were to be streamlined, while the remainder would reveal exactly what was hidden beneath that cloak of steel cladding carried by the 'streamliners'. These five new non-streamlined locomotives made an immediate impact, as their graceful appearance and size won plaudits from many quarters. *Duchess of Sutherland* was the fourth of that batch, numbered 6233 and entering traffic in July 1938, allocated to Camden Depot in London.

For the next 27 years No 6233, renumbered 46233 when the railways were nationalised in 1948, provided sterling service for the LMS, then later with British Railways (BR) London Midland Region (LMR). During those years *Duchess of Sutherland* regularly hauled all the premier express trains on the West Coast Main Line, while footplatemen regarded her as a 'strong engine'.

However, the demise of steam traction, and the 'Duchesses' in particular, was signalled by the infamous 'Modernisation Plan' of 1955, which outlined a switch from steam to diesel and electric traction in a decade. Its impact was clearly evident by the early 1960s, with the wholesale introduction of new, but often unreliable, diesel locomotives, while the plan to electrify the West Coast Main Line had resulted in Crewe to Manchester Piccadilly and Liverpool Lime Street being energised by 1962. Meanwhile, work to continue electrification south to

75th ANNIVERSARY To celebrate the 75th anniversary of *Duchess of Sutherland* entering traffic, a weekend special was organised by the PRCLT from Crewe to Perth. On 6 September 2013 No 46233 charges through Coppenhall Moss, just after departing from Crewe, appropriately on the Down Fast! *JW*

Birmingham and Euston was ongoing. The first three 'Duchesses' were withdrawn on 29 December 1962, followed by a further 13 in 1963. At the end of the summer timetable in 1964, the remainder of the class had all been withdrawn and eventually scrapped, except for the three mentioned earlier.

Duchess of Sutherland was placed into store in October 1963 – still serviceable – but did not work again and was finally withdrawn directly from store in February 1964. *Duchess of Hamilton* was withdrawn at the same time, with No 46235 *City of Birmingham* being removed from traffic at a later date, and while the latter locomotive was donated to the city after which it was named, an unlikely source provided a lifeline for the other two survivors.

Their saviour was Sir Billy Butlin, founder of the famous Butlin's Holiday

Introduction

Camp organisation, who wanted to feature the 'golden age of steam' at his various camps, and by 1963 had already acquired 'Royal Scot' No 46100 *Royal Scot* and 'Princess Royal' No 46203 *Princess Margaret Rose* for display at the Skegness and Pwllheli camps respectively. In early 1964 other suitable candidates for display at the Minehead and Heads of Ayr camps were being sought, with Great Western 'King' No 6018 *King Henry VI* and LNER 'A4' No 60014 *Silver Link* the favoured locomotives. However, the Western and Eastern Region authorities both overplayed their hands, because Butlin's considered the asking price to be too high. As a consequence, these two fine locomotives went for scrap.

But that cloud had a silver lining, as Butlin's again turned to the LMR, with the initial acquisition of No 46229 *Duchess of Hamilton*, earmarked for Minehead. This locomotive was notable in that it had been displayed at the New York World's Fair in 1939, as well as touring parts of the USA in the guise of classmate No 6220 *Coronation*. For the Heads of Ayr camp, *Duchess of Sutherland* was chosen. Other than the Scottish connection with the name, it is unclear why No 46233 was specifically selected except perhaps that she was available at the time, having remained at Edge Hill following withdrawal. Moreover, the LMR asking price of £2,500 each was acceptable to Butlin's. Although not a high figure by today's standards, back in 1964 it was sufficient to buy a good-sized semi-detached house.

After a cosmetic repaint into a shade of 'LMS Red' at Crewe Works and the removal of their smoke deflectors, both locomotives were transferred to their new homes, with *Duchess of Sutherland* arriving at Butlin's Heads of Ayr camp at the end of September 1964, ironically coinciding with the time that the remaining active members of the class were withdrawn from service.

The locomotives proved a popular attraction, especially as 'campers' could visit the footplate together with the opportunity to hear the experiences of former enginemen. However, they were not destined to stay with Butlin's for long, as without any cover the salty coastal air was affecting their external appearance, and increasing maintenance costs. Also, by the late 1960s interest in steam locomotives had waned, overtaken by the advent of space travel and men on the moon. It was probably of little surprise when, in 1970, Butlin's decided that it was time to dispose of the locomotives, and suitable homes were sought.

For *Duchess of Sutherland*, that new home from March 1971 was to be at the Bressingham Steam Museum and Gardens in Norfolk, the brainchild of Alan Bloom, a well-known horticulturist and steam enthusiast. At Bressingham, the

JOB DONE Following the completion of the first ten-year overhaul, the PRCLT team line up in front of *Duchess of Sutherland* after the successful light engine test run on 27 March 2012. From left to right, they are John Riley, Simon Scott, Nigel Barber, Barry Wheatley and Malcolm Baker. *JW*

'Duchess' joined *Royal Scot*, which had already been transferred from Butlin's Skegness camp and 'Britannia' No 70013 *Oliver Cromwell* from the National Collection, which had been at Bressingham since 1968. Bressingham had been chosen as it had the necessary skills and experience of maintaining and operating such locomotives along its internal 500-yard stretch of track. It should be remembered that at this time the now highly skilled heritage railway movement was in just an embryonic stage.

A three-year restoration project followed, culminating on 28 May 1974 with No 6233 being steamed for the first time in preservation, and ten years after being withdrawn by BR. The cost of the restoration was estimated at £16,000, then equivalent to the cost of a decent detached house, together with around 20,000 man hours. For the next couple of years *Duchess of Sutherland* operated over the short length of track earning her keep with footplate rides, until a firebox problem brought the steamings to a close and resulted in a return to static display, albeit this time under cover.

The cost of repairs was considered uneconomic, and for next 18 years No 6233 remained a static exhibit at Bressingham. There were a couple of notable events in that period. First, class mate No 46229 *Duchess of Hamilton* was restored to main-line operations by the National Railway Museum in 1980 and, importantly, in 1989 Butlin's decided to divest itself of its steam locomotive legacy, with Bressingham acquiring both *Duchess of Sutherland* and *Royal Scot*.

Then, in August 1993, with the remaining time on *Duchess of Hamilton*'s second main-line ticket running down, interest again turned to *Duchess of Sutherland*, starting with Bressingham agreeing to release her on loan to the East Lancashire Railway (ELR). Initially for a period of four weeks, it was to be nearly a year before No 6233 returned to Norfolk, the extended period being due to the ELR trying to tie up what proved to be an abortive ten-year loan deal that included a restoration package.

In retrospect, maybe this sudden activity after such a long period of dormancy set a 'train of events' into motion as No 6233 was a valued and valuable but non-performing asset for Bressingham. Of note, an unrelated connection with the Princess Royal Class Locomotive Trust (PRCLT) had been established, who had coincidentally by this time restored another former Butlin's Stanier 'Pacific', 'Princess Royal' Class No 46203 *Princess Margaret Rose*, to main-line condition.

In 1995 the Great Central Railway (GCR) enquired of a possible loan arrangement for No 6233, and with this in the background the trustees of Bressingham Steam Museum deliberated and eventually took the difficult decision to sell *Duchess of Sutherland*. In view of the established connection and its track record of already having restored No 46203, the PRCLT was approached with a view to the Trust purchasing *Duchess of Sutherland*. They were offered 'first refusal', and for the trustees of PRCLT the decision to take up the offer and purchase No 6233 was an easy one.

After an emotional farewell from Bressingham, *Duchess of Sutherland* arrived at her new home, the recently completed PRCLT's West Shed at Swanwick Junction, at Midland Railway-Butterley, on 4 February 1996, and another chapter in the Life and Times of No 6233 *Duchess of Sutherland* commenced. There was the business of financing the purchase, and a successful application to the Heritage Lottery Fund resulted in the Trust receiving a grant of £324,508, which represented 75% of the purchase price and the cost of restoration. Work commenced in late 1998, with the boiler being overhauled at the Severn Valley Railway while most of the remaining work was accomplished 'in-house'.

On 17 January 2001, a nearly complete *Duchess of Sutherland* was positioned outside The West Shed with a fire lit for the first time to gently raise steam and start the running-in process, which was accomplished on the home metals of the Midland Railway-Butterly prior to a formal return to the main line. This took place on 4 July 2001 with a 'light engine' test run, followed by a loaded test run two weeks later, which was not without drama! But the important certificate was issued, and *Duchess of Sutherland* was now able to return to main-line duties after a gap of 38 years.

As well as returning to old haunts, *Duchess of Sutherland* has also visited many pastures new, as well as operating a couple of trains for very special passengers. Now, after two decades back on the main line, *Duchess of Sutherland* is still doing the job that Stanier and Coleman designed her for, climbing challenging grades and fast running, when allowed. The main-line activity for the locomotive in recent years may have resulted in the South Devon Banks of Whiteball, Dainton, Rattery and Hemerdon replacing those of Grayrigg, Shap and Beattock, but no matter where the destination, the 'Duchess' has flattened them all! Not bad for an octogenarian!

LMS and British Railways

SHREWSBURY This very early photograph of *Duchess of Sutherland* in the service of the London Midland & Scottish Railway (LMS) was taken in 1938, possibly on a running-in turn when new from Crewe Works. It is easy to appreciate why these non-streamlined locomotives made such a positive impact with observers of the day. Their dimensions challenged the LMS loading gauge to the limit in order to accommodate their power, epitomised by the large firebox and boiler barrel, along with the bulbous front end. *Rail On-Line*

Left: **LONDON EUSTON** In mid-1948 *Duchess of Sutherland* is now in LMS lined black livery, but still carries her LMS number 6233. The new British Railways number 46233 (i.e. the LMS number plus 40000) was applied in September 1948. Alongside is rebuilt 'Patriot' No 45514 *Holyhead*, which has already been renumbered by this time. Note also that *Duchess of Sutherland* now has a double chimney, installed in 1941, together with smoke deflectors that had been fitted in 1946 to counter the problem of drifting exhaust. *Rail On-Line*

Below: **CALTHWAITE** is north of Penrith, and *Duchess of Sutherland* is heading the Up 'Royal Scot' in 1938, probably soon after being released into traffic. Two LNWR 'Cove Roof' six-wheel vans are positioned behind the tender, which were used for perishable produce. This viewpoint emphasises the excellent proportions of the locomotive and perfectly conveys the grace and power for which they became renowned. *E. E. Smith, Rail Archive Stephenson*

NEWBOLD TROUGHS were north of Rugby on the Trent Valley Line, and *Duchess of Sutherland* is taking water while working an up express sometime in the mid-1950s. The cascading water from the tender is likely a consequence of the fireman not lifting the water scoop quickly enough when the tender had been fully topped up. *Rail On-Line*

TEBAY On 11 August 1958 *Duchess of Sutherland* is about to dig in for the arduous climb to Shap Summit while heading the down 'Lakes Express'. Tebay No 1 signal box can be seen in the distance. Tebay shed was allocated a stud of locomotives to provide banking assistance for freights and some passenger workings, when required, to Shap Summit. In this instance, however, the driver of *Duchess of Sutherland* will not be summoning their assistance. *Gavin Morrison*

Into preservation: from Crewe to Butlin's and Bressingham

Right: **CREWE WORKS** In late August 1964 14-year-old Peter Leigh, using a Kodak Brownie Cresta 120 box camera, captured this view of *Duchess of Sutherland*, now in cosmetic LMS 'red' livery and shorn of the LMS-fitted smoke deflectors. Next stop, Butlins!
Peter Leigh

Below: **NEWTON JUNCTION** signal box, in the right background, was built to give the signalman a good view of the junction beyond the road bridge and Newton-on-Ayr station. It is mid-October 1964 and *Duchess of Sutherland* is stabled in the yard, with a diesel shunter attached in place of the tender, awaiting transfer to Butlin's. Passing is a coal train hauled by 'Crab' 2-6-0 No 42780. *Derek Cross*

Below right: **BUTLIN'S, HEADS OF AYR** *Duchess of Sutherland* is now on a Pickford's trailer, being manoeuvred into the holiday camp. It had been necessary to tranship No 6233 from rail to road at the nearby Greenan Sidings.
Derek Cross

Above: **ALLOWAY JUNCTION** is south of Ayr, and on 21 October 1964 *Duchess of Sutherland* is now sandwiched between diesel shunters Nos D2434 and D3005 as the convoy takes the branch line to Heads of Ayr. At the time it was thought that this would be the last journey on BR metals for No 6233. *Derek Cross*

Above: **BUTLIN'S, HEADS OF AYR** *Duchess of Sutherland* is now on display at the holiday camp together with former London, Brighton & South Coast Railway Class 'A1X' 'Terrier' No 32662 *Martello*. *Derek Cross*

Below: **AYR** The truncated branch to Heads of Ayr closed in 1968, so *Duchess of Sutherland*'s return journey to Ayr was by road. Here, under the watchful eye of the local constabulary, the locomotive is manoeuvred in front of Ayr Grammar School on the way into Townhead Coal Sidings Yard on 24 February 1971, where the transfer to rail will take place. *Derek Cross*

Above: **BUTLIN'S, HEADS OF AYR** *Duchess of Sutherland* is showing the signs of more than six years of exposure to the sea air. With maintenance costs rising and interest in steam declining, it was time to move on. Bressingham Steam Museum was the location of choice, and a new life beckoned. The hawser to draw No 6233 onto the low-loader is in place. Note the banner attached to the boiler grab rail advertising the move. *Derek Cross*

Below: **AYR** Near Blackhouse Junction, later that same day, *Duchess of Sutherland*, now reunited with her tender, is being propelled towards the motive power depot by diesel shunter No D3278. Note that the banner is now gathered in and secured around the boiler grab rail. *Derek Cross*

Locomotives and Recollections: No 6233 *Duchess of Sutherland*

BRESSINGHAM STEAM MUSEUM was the home of *Duchess of Sutherland* from 1971 until 1996, during which time an overhaul took place and the locomotive returned to steam for a couple of years to operate along the short running line. This fascinating photograph shows *Duchess of Sutherland*, the subject of many admiring glances, during her time in steam in the mid-1970s.
Michael Alderman

SWAFFHAM On 3 February 1996 *Duchess of Sutherland* is tethered onto a low-loader and being given a police escort through the busy market place en route from Bressingham to her new home at The West Shed, on what is now the Midland Railway-Butterley. To the left is the Buttercross, erected in 1783 and topped with a statute of the roman goddess Ceres, while to the right in the former Corn Hall, built in 1858. *Howard Routledge*

The West Shed

Above: **BUTTERLEY** After arrival from Bressingham, *Duchess of Sutherland* is positioned in her new home, The West Shed, alongside No 46203 *Princess Margaret Rose*, which had recently been withdrawn from traffic due to boiler problems. *Howard Routledge*

Above right: **BUTTERLEY** After being first steamed in January 2001, a process of running-in at the Midland Railway-Butterley commenced, culminating on 23 May with *Duchess of Sutherland* hauling stock for the first time. Here she is seen propelling the stock along the connection from The West Shed onto the heritage line. *JW*

Right: **BUTTERLEY** *Duchess of Sutherland*, operating tender-first, departs from Swanwick Junction on her first run towards Butterley, passing the impressive former Midland Railway signal box that was rescued from Kettering Station. *JW*

Locomotives and Recollections: No 6233 *Duchess of Sutherland*

MAIN LINE TEST RUNS To obtain a main-line certificate two successful test runs were required. The first was a 'light engine' operation, which on the day also included the PRCLT's support coach together with the 1927 LMS Directors Saloon. This was then followed by a 'loaded' test, which involved hauling a consist equivalent to a normal loading when in traffic. The light engine run took place on 4 July 2001, consisting of two round trips between Derby and Sheffield. The day got off to a bad start with a 2-hour delay due to points problems accessing the main line at Codnor Park Junction, but thereafter it became a perfect day. The loaded test on 18 July was again between Derby and Sheffield with a train consisting of 14 coaches with paying passengers. All was going well until on the last leg back to Derby a sudden brake application near Dronfield brought the train to a stand, bringing the outing to an untimely end. The problem, a minor issue with the new air brake mechanism, was soon identified and remedied the next day, and the 'Duchess' was duly certified to operate on the national network.

On the left *Duchess of Sutherland* approaches Trowell Junction, on the Erewash Valley Line, with the first 'light engine' test run, and then is seen *(below)* having just arrived at Derby station, with the train ready for the loaded test run to Sheffield. *Both JW*

The West Coast Main Line

LONDON EUSTON We begin this illustrated review of *Duchess of Sutherland*'s return to main-line operations on the route for which she and her classmates were specifically designed and built – the West Coast Main Line (WCML). The start point is London Euston, the route's southern terminus, which has been totally rebuilt since the withdrawal of No 46233 in 1964. On 9 July 2004 *Duchess of Sutherland* stands in the 'new' Euston awaiting departure at the head of 'The Mancunian', a Pathfinder Tours charter train to Manchester, via the Trent Valley and Crewe. The high spot was being routed fast line through Nuneaton, at speed, then continuing fast line all the way to Crewe. This part of the station is now being rebuilt again to accommodate the new High Speed 2 line services. *JW*

Right: **WOLVERTON** *Duchess of Sutherland* is eased through the reverse curve on the approach to the station while heading a Steam Dreams charter from Rugby to Bristol on 4 September 2015. *JW*

Below: **HILLMORTON JUNCTION**, on the eastern fringe of Rugby, is where the Northampton Loop rejoins the WCML. On 15 September 2015 *Duchess of Sutherland* is seen passing over the WCML while working off the loop with a Steam Dreams Euston to Penrith charter. *JW*

Below right: **RUGBY** On a damp day *Duchess of Sutherland* gently reverses onto the stock of the Steam Dreams charter to Bristol seen above later in the day at Wolverton. Notable in this view is the nondescript Network Rail Rugby Signalling Centre building on the right. *JW*

The West Coast Main Line

Right: **RUGELEY TRENT VALLEY** With the ghostly outline of the cooling towers at Rugeley Power Station forming a backdrop, *Duchess of Sutherland*, now in LMS black livery, works hard on the approach to the station while heading for Chester with a Steam Dreams 'Cathedrals Express' charter from Euston on 9 October 2010. JW

Left: **LICHFIELD** On 9 May 2014 *Duchess of Sutherland* approaches Trent Valley station at speed while heading a Steam Dreams London Victoria to Appleby charter. This section of the WCML, between Tamworth and Armitage, had been upgraded from double to quadruple track six years earlier. JW

STAFFORD This was the view looking back into the station from the now closed Stafford No 5 signal box on 14 June 2013, as *Duchess of Sutherland* and support coach approach with a positioning move from Swanwick Junction to Crewe ahead of a main-line duty. *Richard Tuplin*

STOKE ON TRENT station was built by the North Staffordshire Railway and crowned with a superb glazed 'ridge and furrow' roof. On 19 April 2003 *Duchess of Sutherland* is suitably highlighted by spring sunshine as she passes with the PMR Tours 'Coronation Tower' from Chesterfield to Blackpool North. *JW*

The West Coast Main Line

CREWE was the birthplace and spiritual home of the 'Duchesses'. It is, then, always a special occasion when *Duchess of Sutherland* visits, as the station is just a short distance from the works where she was built in 1938. On 20 April 2002 the locomotive is seen easing out of Platform 12 at the head of the PMR Tours 'Citadel Express' to Carlisle via Shap. On the left is an Inter City-liveried Class 86 electric locomotive, which were introduced in 1966 and became worthy successors to the 'Princess Coronations'. Note, too, the date, which is of significance as less than two months later No 6233 had an appointment with a Very Important Person (see pages 54-56) *JW*

PRESTON *Duchess of Sutherland* simmers at the head of the Railway Touring Company's (RTC) 'The Mid-Day Scot' on 19 March 2016, having just arrived from Manchester Victoria. The destination is Edinburgh Waverley, but for many of the passengers the highlight will be travelling behind a 'Duchess' over 'home territory', and particularly the ascents of Grayrigg, then Shap and finally Beattock. Note the fine roof at Preston, whose first station opened in 1838, while the current edifice dates back to 1880. *JW*

LANCASTER A damp 9 April 2007 is certainly brightened by the sight of *Duchess of Sutherland* storming through the station heading RTC's 'Great Britain' from Preston to Glasgow Central. This round-Britain charter train, featuring several different locomotives, had left London Paddington three days earlier, and was due back into London King's Cross some nine days later, during which time it will have visited Penzance and Wick and many points in between! *JW*

HEST BANK After taking water at nearby Carnforth, *Duchess of Sutherland* is now accelerating through Hest Bank on the final leg of the PMR Tours 'Citadel Express' from Carlisle to Crewe on 3 June 2006. Hest Bank signal box and level crossing are located on the far side of the footbridge. *JW*

DILLICAR COMMON In this panoramic view across the valley of the River Lune on 8 May 2010, *Duchess of Sutherland* heads north with the PMR Tours 'Citadel Express' from Gloucester to Carlisle. The train has just passed Lowgill and is heading onto just over a mile of level track, once the site of Dillicar water troughs, before the gradient again stiffens for the climb through Tebay to Shap Summit. The troughs were just over 500 yards long, so on a fast-moving train the fireman had to be precise in his timing when lowering then retracting the water scoop to ensure a fully topped-up tender. *JW*

Left: **GREENHOLME** is on the climb to Shap Summit, where the gradient has now stiffened to a punishing 1 in 75 for the remaining 4 miles to the top. On 9 April 2007 sunshine has followed a heavy shower just in time to highlight a storming ascent of Shap by *Duchess of Sutherland*, heading the 'Great Britain' tour seen earlier at Lancaster. Tebay, and traffic on the M6 motorway, can be seen on the far left. *JW*

Right: **SCOUT GREEN** signal box was positioned around the mid-point of the climb to Shap, and served to break the section between Tebay and the summit, as well as controlling a level crossing over a minor road. It closed in 1973, but had already gained legendary status for the army of spotters and photographers who recorded the last days of steam in the 1950s and '60s. On 10 October 2009 *Duchess of Sutherland* offers a reminder of those halcyon days as she approaches Scout Green heading a charter working for RTC from Euston to Carlisle. *JW*

Above left: **SHAP** *Duchess of Sutherland* has just breasted the summit following the longer but slightly easier southbound climb from Penrith while heading a returning PMR Tours Carlisle to Gloucester 'Citadel Express' on 8 May 2010. *JW*

Above: **BESSIE GHYLL**, near Thrimby Grange, is the location on 28 March 2009 as *Duchess of Sutherland* passes on the climb to Shap, heading the returning RTC 'Cumbrian Mountain Express' charter to Worcester. No 6233 had earlier worked the train north from Hellifield to Carlisle over the Settle & Carlisle line. *JW*

Left: **GREAT STRICKLAND** is south of Penrith, and here *Duchess of Sutherland* is being worked hard on the southbound climb to Shap Summit on 17 June 2006 while heading a returning RTC Carlisle-Euston charter. *JW*

CARLISLE, the 'Border City', is seen on 27 September 2003, as *Duchess of Sutherland* simmers in the platform at Carlisle Citadel station taking water while working the PMR Tours 'Coronation Scot' from Manchester Victoria to Glasgow Central. The run north had not been without incident, because of a problem with an injector during the ascent to Shap Summit, which initially reduced the train to walking pace, then finally to a stand just short of the summit. It is reported that a few judicial blows with a large spanner rectified the issue, as No 6233 was again soon on the move without further problem, which included easily restarting the train on the 1 in 75 adverse gradient to the summit. *JW*

The Settle & Carlisle line

ARMATHWAITE is the first station on the Settle & Carlisle line (S&C) south from Carlisle. It opened in 1876, and the original station building (left) survives in private hands. It was closed in May 1970 when the local stopping service was withdrawn, then reopened in 1986. On 8 September 2007 *Duchess of Sutherland*'s fireman is laying down an effective smoke screen as his train hurries through the attractive station while working south with the RTC 'Hadrian' charter from York. The 'Royal Scot' headboard is for show only! *JW*

NEWBIGGIN is a Cumbrian village south of Culgaith. Its station closed in May 1970, and while the original building survives in private hands the platforms have been demolished. *Duchess of Sutherland* is seen approaching the site of the former station on 22 May 2013, heading a returning RTC 'Cumbrian Mountain Express' from Carlisle to Euston. The train has just passed beneath the graceful three-arched occupation bridge, while the abutments of Crowdundle Viaduct can just be seen to the left of the rear coaches. *JW*

APPLEBY This attractive market town is a destination in its own right, and for southbound steam excursions a place to take water, with the prospect of the 'Long Drag' to Ais Gill summit ahead. A water tower and water crane have been specifically provided for this purpose. On 18 October 2014 *Duchess of Sutherland* draws into the station in anticipation of taking water with the southbound 'Thames Clyde Express', a PMR Tours charter returning to Leicester from Carlisle. *JW*

The Settle & Carlisle line

CROSBY GARRETT VIADUCT is located a little less than halfway along the daunting climb of 15 miles from Ormside to the summit at Ais Gill, known as the 'Long Drag'. *Duchess of Sutherland* is seen working across the attractive viaduct, which overshadows the village from which it takes its name, with the PMR Tours 'Thames Clyde Express' seen earlier at Appleby *(page 26)*. JW

SMARDALE Here the ruling gradient is 1 in 100, and looks to be taxing *Duchess of Sutherland*'s fireman judging by the colour of the exhaust blasting from her chimney. There is still much hard work to be done as Ais Gill summit is still some 8 miles of hard climbing away. The train is the final leg of the RTC's 2012 'Great Britain V' tour from Glasgow to Preston on 26 April 2012. JW

BIRKETT COMMON, south of Kirkby Stephen, affords wonderful panoramic views of the Pennine Chain. Often referred to as the 'Roof of England', the Pennines stretch from the Peak District in Derbyshire to the Tyne Gap close to the border with Scotland. On 22 May 2013 *Duchess of Sutherland* is seen passing through this splendid vista while heading the 'Cumbrian Mountain Express' from Carlisle to Euston previously seen at Newbiggin (page 26). JW

AIS GILL at last, and *Duchess of Sutherland*'s fireman will shortly be able to relax, as the 'Long Drag' is nearly done. Ais Gill summit, which is 1,169 feet above sea level and the highest point on the S&C, is just a short distance away. Wild Boar Fell provides an imposing backdrop as No 6233 heads the PMR Tours 'Carlisle Coronation' from Carlisle to Crewe on 3 July 2004. JW

The Settle & Carlisle line

GARSDALE station, formerly known as Hawes Junction, is actually located at Garsdale Head, a few miles from the village after which it is named. It is in a remote, exposed spot, perched on the side of the valley – so exposed, in fact, that there was once a turntable located there and during one particular storm the shed pilot locomotive, positioned on the turntable, was spun around by the force of the gale. There was to such problem for *Duchess of Sutherland* on 18 October 2014, seen here breezing through the station heading the outward PMR Tours 'Thames Clyde Express'. *JW*

RIBBLEHEAD With early evening sunshine glinting off her paintwork, *Duchess of Sutherland* approaches the station on 8 September 2007, heading back to York with the RTC's 'Hadrian' charter. This was a circular working from York that had earlier operated along the Tyne Valley line via Hexham to Carlisle. The 2,415-foot peak of Whernside provides an impressive backdrop. *JW*

Right: **HELLIFIELD SOUTH JUNCTION**'s signalman gets a friendly wave from the crew of *Duchess of Sutherland* as they work No 46233 off the line from Blackburn and enter the goods loop to take water. The train is the RTC's 'Cumbrian Mountain Express' from Liverpool Lime Street to Carlisle on 1 August 2015. *JW*

Below: **GISBURN** signal box, on the line from Blackburn to Hellifield, closed in 1981, but has survived and the structure is now in private hands. On 18 July 2015 *Duchess of Sutherland* passes the site of the former station, which closed in 1962, heading another RTC 'Cumbrian Mountain Express', again from Liverpool Lime Street to Carlisle. *JW*

Left: **BAMBER BRIDGE** station level crossing frame is now encased in a 'Meccano'-style framework of steel girders, which also span the running lines, to provide support for the three-storey structure that dates back to 1906. This was the scene well before structural weaknesses were identified, with *Duchess of Sutherland* passing at the head of the PMR Tours 'Carlisle Coronation' returning to Leicester on 3 July 2004. *JW*

The North West

OLIVE MOUNT CUTTING The deep cuttings at Edge Hill and Olive Mount are notable features of the line from Lime Street station. The 2-mile-long Olive Mount Cutting was completed in 1830 when trains operated to Liverpool's first station at Crown Street. It is 80 feet deep, originally excavated for a two-track railway, but later enlarged to accommodate a four-track formation in 1871. The view seen here is now significantly changed following electrification. *Duchess of Sutherland* has just passed through Wavertree Technology Park station on 27 July 2013, heading an RTC 'Cumbrian Mountain Express' to Carlisle. Diverging on the right is the branch to Bootle, which serves the docks. Note Liverpool's Roman Catholic Cathedral in the background. *JW*

EDGE HILL CUTTING was originally a 1,060-metre tunnel to the then new Lime Street station, which opened in 1836, replacing Crown Street, which subsequently closed. Originally catering for two tracks, the tunnel was later opened out and the resulting deep cutting enlarged to cater for an extra pair of running lines. A number of 'short' tunnels remain, which act as buttresses supporting the cutting walls, as well as providing for road crossings and buildings. Here we are looking into the cutting from Edge Hill station on 8 August 2010, as *Duchess of Sutherland* approaches with the RTC's 'North Wales Coast Express' to Holyhead. *JW*

BLACKPOOL is the recreational Mecca of the North West, and has long been a popular destination of excursion trains. In recent years *Duchess of Sutherland* has visited the resort on a number of occasions, one such being on 19 April 2003, with PMR Tours' aptly named 'Coronation Tower' from Derby. Here the train is seen departing from Blackpool North on the return journey, with the iconic Tower in the background. This structure was completed in 1894 and is 518 feet tall. Also of note is the former Lancashire & Yorkshire Railway signal box on the right, which then controlled all movements into and out of the station. It was closed and demolished in 2017 when the Fylde Line was resignalled, electrified and the station area remodelled. *JW*

The North West

Right: **POULTON-LE-FYLDE** On 5 June 2010 *Duchess of Sutherland* 'has the road' to Blackpool North at the head of the PMR Tours 'Fylde Coast Express' from Sheffield. The bracket signal controls the junction, just beyond the station, where the Blackpool and Fleetwood lines diverged. The latter is now closed, but subject to a preservation scheme. *JW*

Below: **KIRKHAM & WESHAM** has been subject to much change since this scene was captured on 16 June 2012, as a result of electrification. On that day *Duchess of Sutherland* approaches on the now lifted former through lines heading the returning PMR Tours 'Fylde Coast Express' to Sheffield. *JW*

Below right: **SALWICK**, the first station on the Fylde Line from Preston, is now a shadow of its former self and is currently served by just two return peak-hour trains each weekday.
On 5 June 2010 *Duchess of Sutherland* is seen passing at speed with the return 'Fylde Coast Express' seen above on the outward journey at Poulton-le-Fylde. *JW*

MANCHESTER The 'Castlefield Corridor' is the name given to a short but very congested stretch of railway running from Manchester Piccadilly, through Oxford Road station to Deansgate. The double-track section between Piccadilly and Oxford Road stations is carried along a low viaduct, and passes alongside the campus of Manchester University. On 30 August 2014 *Duchess of Sutherland* heads away from Piccadilly along the viaduct with an RTC 'Cumbrian Mountain Express' from Crewe to Carlisle. *JW*

MANCHESTER is the scene on 13 June 2004, with its impressive skyline providing a backdrop to *Duchess of Sutherland*, which is heading a Northern Belle Luncheon circular from Manchester Victoria towards Salford. The train was routed via Blackburn and Settle Junction, prior to returning to Manchester by way of the scenic 'Little North Western Line' through Wennington before joining the West Coast Main Line at Carnforth. *JW*

The North Wales Coast Line

HOLYHEAD, terminus and ferry port – change here for Ireland! In steam days it was the destination of such well-known services as the 'Irish Mail' and 'Emerald Isle Express'. It has also been a frequent destination for *Duchess of Sutherland* over the years, but this working on 18 June 2005 turned out to be exceptional as the train was signalled into Platform 2, under the roof, instead of the more usual outside platform. Due to the curvature of the platform the approach was made with extreme caution as the clearance between locomotive and platform edge was very tight. Note, too, that the typical LNWR-style roof renders this scene very reminiscent of an arrival at the old Euston station. The train is the PMR Tours 'Welsh Dragon Relief' from Northampton. The headboard celebrates the bicentenary of renowned civil engineering contractor Thomas Brassey, who built the Chester to Holyhead Railway, opened in 1845, together with many other lines both in the UK and worldwide. *JW*

Locomotives and Recollections: No 6233 *Duchess of Sutherland*

Main picture: **VALLEY** is the first station from Holyhead, some 5 miles distant. It is also the location of the loading point for nuclear flasks from the now decommissioned Wylfa Power Station. In the 1980s the access to the loading point was expanded to incorporate a triangle to turn steam locomotives, and part of this can be seen in the background as *Duchess of Sutherland* passes on 8 August 2010, heading the returning RTC 'North Wales Coast Express' to Liverpool Lime Street. *JW*

Left inset: **BODORGAN** A cheery wave and the clicks of a few cameras greet *Duchess of Sutherland*, speeding through the impressive stone-built station on 19 May 2012 heading for Holyhead with the PMR Tours 'Welsh Dragon' from Bristol Temple Meads. *JW*

LLANFAIRPWLL Also known as Llanfair PG, both the shortened versions of the very, very long name that can be seen attached to the station building. However, on 19 May 2012 *Duchess of Sutherland* is the attraction, seen coasting through the station in readiness for crossing the nearby Menai Strait on the rebuilt Britannia Bridge. This is the return 'Welsh Dragon' charter, seen earlier passing Bodorgan on the outward working. *JW*

LLANFAIRFECHAN is where the main line is sandwiched between the sea and the A55 trunk road. Between here and Penmaenmawr the railway is built on a ledge above the sea, and offers panoramic views of Conwy Bay, and particularly the Great Orme. The latter forms a backdrop to *Duchess of Sutherland* as she heads for Holyhead from Liverpool Lime Street with an RTC 'North Wales Coast Express' on 8 August 2010. *JW*

PENMAENMAWR can be seen in the background as *Duchess of Sutherland* works along the coast and is about to enter the short Penmaenbach Tunnel on 2 August 2009, while heading the returning RTC 'North Wales Coast Express' to Liverpool Lime Street. The coastline of Anglesey is prominent on the horizon. *JW*

LLANDUDNO is situated at the end of a 3-mile branch from Llandudno Junction, and is the site of one of the last remaining semaphore signal gantries on the national network. On 8 August 2010 *Duchess of Sutherland* pulls into the station with the 'North Wales Coast Express' from Liverpool Lime Street to Holyhead. *JW*

Above: **MOSTYN** station closed in 1966, although the building survives in private hands and can just be seen to the right of the Grade II-listed signal box that controls access to the adjacent dock. Passing on 24 April 2010, *Duchess of Sutherland* heads the returning PMR Tours 'Red Dragon' charter to Lincoln. *JW*

Right: **CHESTER** is famous for many things, one being the home of the oldest operation race course known as 'The Rondee'. The course and city skyline provide a backdrop to *Duchess of Sutherland*, which is working away from the city heading across the viaduct named after the race course and heading for Holyhead with the RTC's 'North Wales Coast Express' on 8 August 2010. *JW*

Above: **LLANDUDNO JUNCTION** A very tight curve running around the back gardens of terraced properties takes the Llandudno branch onto the main line from Holyhead. On 8 August 2010 *Duchess of Sutherland* is returning from Llandudno, and being carefully eased through that curve before rejoining the main line while working the returning 'North Wales Coast Express' to Liverpool Lime Street seen earlier in the day at Llandudno station. *JW*

The Welsh Borders

Right: **TRAM INN** On 29 April 2019 *Duchess of Sutherland* paid a rare visit to the 'Welsh Marches Line' to head the Taunton to Preston section of the RTC's 'Great Britain XII' tour. This line runs along the border of England and Wales from Newport to Wrexham, and the following three views reflect the progress of the train along this historic route.

The first is at Tram Inn, between Hereford and Pontrilas, where the station closed in 1958 but the signal box remains to control a busy level crossing. The line is still manually signalled, and offers the unusual sight of *Duchess of Sutherland* and Great Western lower-quadrant signals. *JW*

Left: **CHIRK** is notable for two very distinctive viaducts that span the Ceiriog Valley on the southern approach to the town. Thomas Telford built his aqueduct for the Ellesmere Canal in 1801, which can just be seen through the second arch of the 1848 railway viaduct constructed by Thomas Brassey. *Duchess of Sutherland*, heading 'GBXII', has just passed from England into Wales, as the border follows the River Ceiriog. *JW*

Right: **MORETON-ON-LUGG** station, located north of Hereford, was another closure in 1958, although the building survives and is in private hands. The RTC's 'GBXII' working has been checked because of reports of trespassers on the line, and the signal has just cleared in *Duchess of Sutherland*'s favour. *JW*

The Midlands

Right: **SHREWSBURY**, strategically placed on the fringe of the border between the Midlands and Wales, is also a major railway junction with widespread important connections. It is also one of the last outposts of manual signalling, with active signal boxes at Crewe Junction, Sutton Bridge and the two illustrated here, Abbey Foregate and Severn Bridge Junction, the latter being the largest operational mechanical signal box in the world. *Duchess of Sutherland* has just weaved through Abbey Foregate Junction, and is now heading for Wolverhampton on 13 August 2017 with a Steam Dreams charter from Crewe to London Paddington. *JW*

Below: **SHIFNAL VIADUCT**'s 12 arches carry the line from Shrewsbury to Wolverhampton high above the rooftops of the market town, and no doubt the passengers on this Northern Belle Luncheon Circular, hauled throughout by *Duchess of Sutherland* from Birmingham International via Crewe and Chester on 26 June 2003, are enjoying that view, as well as their lunch. *JW*

Below right: **ALBRIGHTON** station's Great Western heritage has been preserved virtually intact. However, word of a steam special has obviously got out, as a crowd of onlookers cheer the passage of *Duchess of Sutherland*, heading the charter seen above passing Abbey Foregate on 13 August 2017. *JW*

The Midlands

Left: **WILLENHALL**, renowned for the manufacture of locks and keys, is situated on the Grand Junction line from Stafford to Birmingham, avoiding Wolverhampton. On 19 July 2008 *Duchess of Sutherland* passes the former Yale Lock Factory, now owned by the Swedish Assa Abloy Company, heading for London Paddington with a Steam Dreams 'Cathedrals Express' from Chester. *JW*

Top right: **WALSALL**'s Grade II-listed Town Hall, with its distinctive tower, is a local landmark. *Duchess of Sutherland*, having taken water at Walsall station, is seen approaching Ryecroft Junction at the head of the Steam Dreams charter seen earlier at Willenhall. *JW*

Right: **HAMSTEAD** station, formerly known as Great Barr, is located on the Grand Junction line between Tame Bridge Parkway and Perry Barr stations. This is the Steam Dreams excursion seen earlier at Abbey Foregate Junction and Albrighton, with *Duchess of Sutherland* now working through the Birmingham suburbs en route to London Paddington. *JW*

Left: **BURTON-UPON-TRENT** is the brewery capital of the UK, where the large Coors complex, with its distinct silos, overshadows the town's station. Note, too, the wide island platform that formerly housed a large and impressive station building. On 29 March 2012 *Duchess of Sutherland* is seen working non-stop through the station at the head of a public loaded test run after overhaul from Derby to Crewe and back via Lichfield and Stafford. It was a notable event, being the locomotive's first public outing in BR green livery and numbered 46233. *JW*

Below: **WHITACRE JUNCTION** *Duchess of Sutherland* approaches at the head of the returning PMR Tours 'Oxfordshire Express' from Didcot to Manchester Victoria on 23 May 2015. This location is notable for the magnificent edifice of Whitacre Waterworks Pumping House, built in 1872 and apparently an example of 'Victorian Civic Gospel' architectural design. *JW*

Below: **BURTON-UPON-TRENT** The large former Midland Railway Stores and Grain Warehouse and the now demolished Coors Tower provide a historical perspective to Burton-upon-Trent as *Duchess of Sutherland* passes alongside the numerous classes of diesel locomotives stabled at the Nemesis Rail Depot. It is working the Vintage Trains 'Scarborough Flyer' from Tyseley on 30 June 2012. *JW*

WASHWOOD HEATH Sidings No 1 signal box had recently been decommissioned, although externally it remained in a decent state of repair, if you ignore the ominous lean to the right of course! Passing, and no doubt loosening the signal box foundations further, is *Duchess of Sutherland* on 30 June 2012, heading the Vintage Trains 'Scarborough Flyer' from Tyseley. On the left is a Network Rail Rail Grinding Train, which reprofiles worn or damaged rail heads. JW

BIRMINGHAM city centre, with the notable landmarks of the Rotunda, the Selfridges building and the BT Tower, provides a panoramic backdrop as *Duchess of Sutherland* approaches Small Heath station on 23 May 2015, heading the PMR Tours 'Oxfordshire Express' from Manchester Victoria to Didcot. JW

Right: **BENTLEY HEATH** level crossing is just north of Dorridge, which *Duchess of Sutherland* approaches at speed at the head of the returning Vintage Trains 'Shakespeare Express' from Stratford-upon-Avon seen in the previous picture *(left)*. *JW*

Below: **LEAMINGTON SPA** *Duchess of Sutherland* accelerates along the low viaduct leading from the station, after a pathing stop, while heading the Vintage Trains 'Whistling Ghost V' from Solihull to Minehead on 17 June 2017. The viaduct on the right once carried the now closed LMS line from Rugby. *JW*

Above: **TYSELEY** Steam Trust's premises and workshops can be seen in the background, sandwiched between the main-line motive power depot and maintenance facility. On 2 September 2007 *Duchess of Sutherland* is seen working from the steam depot with empty coaching stock for Birmingham Snow Hill, prior to working the Vintage Trains 'Shakespeare Express' to Stratford-upon-Avon. *JW*

The Midlands

STECHFORD On a damp 22 November 2014 *Duchess of Sutherland* works off the line from Aston, and joins the main line to Rugby and the WCML. The chord from Aston is very useful as it enables through workings to avoid having to pass through the congested Birmingham New Street station, and is particularly useful for diversions when the Trent Valley Line is closed. The train is the PMR Tours 'London Explorer' from Sheffield to Euston. *JW*

COVENTRY *Duchess of Sutherland* is heading for London Euston with another PMR Tours 'London Explorer', this time from Derby on 14 November 2015. The station was one of many rebuilt when the former London & Birmingham Railway was electrified in the early 1960s, a notable feature being the name and number plate of *Duchess of Sutherland*'s classmate No 46240 *City of Coventry* affixed to a wall on the station footbridge. *JW*

The South Midlands

ECKINGTON BRIDGE carries the former Midland Railway's Birmingham-Bristol main line across the River Avon south of Worcester. It is not a location that would normally be associated with 'Duchesses', but open access to the national network as part of the privatisation package has certainly provided opportunities for such locomotives to operate well outside their 'steam days' boundaries. *Duchess of Sutherland* crossing the River Avon at Eckington is not only a good example of the new system, but also offers a fine sight. The train is a Steam Dreams 'Cathedrals Express' from London Victoria to Worcester on 27 August 2008. *JW*

The South Midlands

Above: **WORCESTER SHRUB HILL** station can be seen in the background as *Duchess of Sutherland* heads for London Victoria on 27 August 2008, working the return Steam Dreams 'Cathedrals Express' charter. Together with Shrewsbury (see page 40), Worcester remains one of the last outposts of semaphore signalling on the national network. *JW*

Above right: **MORETON-IN-MARSH**, a charming market town on the Cotswold Line, is also controlled by mechanical signalling. On 24 August 2019 *Duchess of Sutherland* heads south non-stop through the station with the returning RTC 'Cotswold Venturer' charter from Worcester Shrub Hill to London Paddington. *JW*

Right: **TWYFORD BRIDGE** is on the former Great Western Paddington to Birmingham main line. It overlooks nearby King's Sutton, and the very distinctive spire of the church of St Peter & St Paul. On 23 May 2015 *Duchess of Sutherland* further enhances the scene, heading the return PMR Tours 'Oxfordshire Explorer' seen earlier at Small Heath (page 43). *JW*

Overhaul

After ten years in traffic, *Duchess of Sutherland* was required to undergo the mandatory general overhaul in order to be recertified for main-line operations. This commenced in November 2010, and was completed in March 2012. Most of the work was undertaken in-house, except for the boiler, which was overhauled at Crewe Heritage Centre. Reassembly took place in October 2011 at The West Shed following the return of the boiler.

This view, looking along the frame from the front buffer beam, shows the caulking on the smokebox saddle ready to accept the reassembled boiler and smokebox, together with the loading chutes for the sanding equipment and the exhaust steam feed pipe to the exhaust injector. JW

The delicate process of lining up and lowering the boiler into position onto the frame and smokebox saddle. JW

NEAR RIPLEY. The boiler being returned from Crewe is seen on the A38 near Ripley. JW

Back inside The West Shed, work is ongoing to connect all the pipework necessary to produce a working steam locomotive. JW

Scotland

GLASGOW CENTRAL is one of the world's great stations. Opened in 1879 by the Caledonian Railway, it is the northern terminus of the West Coast Main Line, the busiest station in Scotland and the 12th busiest in the UK. The imposing structure of today, notable for its large glazed roof and formidable ironwork, is the result of it being rebuilt and expanded between 1901 and 1905. 'Duchesses' were regular visitors on the principal West Coast expresses, and on 27 September 2003 *Duchess of Sutherland* once again graced Glasgow Central and is seen awaiting departure for Manchester Victoria with the PMR Tours 'Caledonian Scot'. Of note, the area to the left, through the arch, has since been returned to rail use with the creation of two new platforms to cater for increased demand. *JW*

Left: **BEATTOCK SUMMIT** is the highest point on the West Coast Main Line, recorded at 1,016 feet above sea level. It is a formidable obstacle, especially for northbound trains, which in steam days often sought the assistance of a banking locomotive for the 10-mile slog from Beattock station to the summit. This was 'Duchess' territory – they were designed to climb the 'northern banks' unassisted with heavy trains, and that they did. On 19 March 2016 *Duchess of Sutherland* is well in charge of 11 bogies, seen running alongside the M74 at Howe Beck with the RTC 'Mid-Day Scot' from Manchester Victoria to Edinburgh Waverley. *JW*

Right: **DUMFRIES** is located on the alternative former Glasgow & South Western Railway line from Glasgow to Carlisle via Kilmarnock, which was a direct competitor of the Caledonian Railway's main line over Beattock. It was also the junction with the 'Port Road', the direct line to Stranraer, which closed in 1965. In BR days 'Duchesses' were a common sight on the route, so on 26 April 2012 *Duchess of Sutherland* is back on familiar territory, easing through the attractive station with the RTC 'Great Britain V' charter, which it was hauling from Glasgow to Preston. *JW*

Scotland

The Forth Circle

FORTH BRIDGE On 14 September 2014 *Duchess of Sutherland* worked two 'Forth Circle' charters for the Scottish Railway Preservation Society (SRPS). Both trains crossed the Firth of Forth on the majestic Forth Bridge before working around Fife via Kirkcaldy, Cowdenbeath and Dunfermline, then ran along the north shore of the Firth of Forth through Culross and Alloa to Stirling. This first view is looking ahead from the footplate as *Duchess of Sutherland* approaches the south portal of the bridge. *Paul Wood*

Above: **FORTH BRIDGE** This colossus, which spans the Firth of Forth between Dalmeny and North Queensferry, opened in 1890, is 8,094 feet long, towers 361 feet above high water, and is one of the most recognisable structures in the world. *Duchess of Sutherland* is seen emerging from the northern portal while heading the morning train from Linlithgow. *JW*

Right: **INVERKEITHING** station is located on a reverse curve, which *Duchess of Sutherland* negotiates with the morning train. Note the towers of the Forth Bridge in the background.
Ian Lothian

The Forth Circle

Right: **CULROSS** After heading around Fife, the charter took the single line from Charlestown Junction to Alloa and Stirling. *Duchess of Sutherland* is seen working along the north shore of the Firth of Forth at Culross, with the distinctive spire of the Town House prominent in the background. JW

Below: **KINCARDINE** This is the view from the approach road to the Kincardine Bridge, looking back towards the now closed and demolished Longannet Power Station. *Duchess of Sutherland* approaches heading for Alloa and Stirling with the SRPS charter train. JW

Below right: **LINLITHGOW BRIDGE** is the location of an impressive 23-arch viaduct, completed in 1842. *Duchess of Sutherland* is being eased across the viaduct in readiness for the forthcoming set-down stop at Linlithgow station on the second working of the day. JW

Scotland

FORTH BRIDGE is illuminated at night, and on 14 September 2014 *Duchess of Sutherland's* exhaust is highlighted while working the final leg of the second 'Forth Circle' charter on that day. The road deck of the first Forth Road Bridge can be seen in the background together with construction work of the new road bridge, which opened in 2017. *JW*

EDINBURGH WAVERLEY station is situated at the heart of the Scottish capital and surrounded by historic buildings. It is itself an iconic structure, with an extensive glazed roof. The Balmoral Hotel, formerly the North British, overlooks the station, with its clock tower prominent; this has always been set 3 minutes fast so that people do not miss their trains, except on 31 December, of course! On 19 March 2016 *Duchess of Sutherland* departs from Waverley with the empty stock of the RTC 'Mid-Day Scot' from Manchester Victoria. *Michael Denholm*

The Royal Train

On 12 June 2002 *Duchess of Sutherland* became the first steam locomotive to haul the Royal Train for 35 years. The working was one component of a tour of North Wales by HM The Queen, organised as part of her Golden Jubilee celebrations. The Royal party had joined the train at Euston the previous evening and travelled overnight to Holyhead, where *Duchess of Sutherland* took over the train from 'Royal' Class 47 No 47787 *Windsor Castle* to draw it forward the couple of miles to the Valley triangle, normally used for loading nuclear flasks from Wyfla Power Station. While the train was stabled at Valley The Queen and HRH Prince Philip were able to prepare for their day of engagements and take breakfast. At the appointed hour the train was drawn forward onto the main line by the Class 47, from where the 'Duchess' again took over for the journey to Llanfairpwll, where the Royal party alighted to commence the day's activities. It then continued on to Bangor, before reversing and returning diesel-hauled to Holyhead to be serviced. Then *Duchess of Sutherland* hauled the ECS to Llandudno Junction, where the Royal party were introduced to the crew before rejoining the train for the final leg to Crewe, where the steam section terminated.

VALLEY Although a wonderfully sunny day, Anglesey was being buffeted by a strong westerly wind, sufficient to push *Duchess of Sutherland*'s exhaust well away from the consist while she lifted the heavy train away from Valley for Llanfairpwll with the Royal party on board. Note the 'crown' headboard, a replica of similar designs carried by BR LMR expresses during the Coronation week in 1953. *JW*

The Royal Train

Right: **VALLEY TRIANGLE** *Duchess of Sutherland* is at the head of the Royal Train next to the nuclear flask loading facility. *JW*

Above right: **VALLEY** Near the RAF base *Duchess of Sutherland* heads the ECS of the Royal Train to Llandudno Junction after the stock had been serviced at Holyhead. *JW*

Right: **BANGOR** *Duchess of Sutherland* leads the ECS from Llanfairpwll from Belmont Tunnel and passes the impressive signal box. The train will later return to Holyhead for servicing. *JW*

Locomotives and Recollections: No 6233 *Duchess of Sutherland*

Left: To mark the occasion the PRCLT presented HM The Queen with a specially produced lamp, handed over by the Trust's chairman Brell Ewart during the line-up for introductions of the train and support crew. The lamp is reported to be mounted on the wall of the Royal Train's Queen's Saloon. *John F. Stiles*

Above: **GARSDALE** *Duchess of Sutherland* works north at Garsdale with its second Royal Train working on 22 March 2005, this time conveying HRH The Prince of Wales from Hellifield to Carlisle as part of the 25th anniversary of the formation of The Friends of the Settle & Carlisle. A headboard displaying the crest of the Prince of Wales was carried on the smokebox door of No 6233. During the journey it was reported that the Prince spent some time on the footplate. *Richard Tuplin*

Heritage lines

The sight of any LMS 'Pacific' on a single-track rural railway would have been unthinkable back in 'steam days', but the preservation movement changed all that and now *Duchess of Sutherland* has been a much valued visitor to a number of heritage lines over recent years.

Below: **MIDLAND RAILWAY-BUTTERLEY** is *Duchess of Sutherland*'s home base. On 20 July 2014 the 'Duchess' is seen arriving at Swanwick Junction, where the PRCLT's West Shed is located, while heading a train for Butterley. The station building once stood at Syston, on the Midland Main Line north of Leicester. *JW*

Right: **SEVERN VALLEY RAILWAY** *Duchess of Sutherland* approaches Kidderminster on 22 September 2002 with a service from Bridgnorth. Note the large carriage shed in the background together with examples of the SVR diesel fleet on the right. *JW*

Below right: **EAST LANCASHIRE RAILWAY** This heritage line runs from Heywood via Bury to Rawtenstall. On 17 October 2012 *Duchess of Sutherland* energetically heads through Irwell Vale station under a threatening sky during a photographers' charter. *JW*

Left: **TYSELEY STEAM TRUST** has entertained *Duchess of Sutherland* on a number of occasions, both to participate in its open days as well as to work charter trains. On 14 July 2014 No 46233 is seen positioned on the turntable that was once part of the old steam depot at Tyseley. *JW*

Below left: **SWANAGE RAILWAY** operates from that charming Dorset coastal resort to Norden via Corfe, and now also has a main-line connection at Wareham. It is usually the preserve of former Southern Railway locomotives, but on 13 October 2018 *Duchess of Sutherland* was the star of the railway's steam gala, seen departing from Corfe station with the ruins of the 11th-century castle built by William the Conqueror in the background. *Dave Robinson*

Left: **MID-NORFOLK RAILWAY** Based at Dereham, this line operates services south to Wymondham Abbey, beyond which there is a main-line connection. *Duchess of Sutherland* has visited the railway on a couple of occasions, and is seen here passing through Yaxham station with a service for Dereham on 25 June 2016. *Ian Williams*

The East Coast Main Line and connections

LONDON KING'S CROSS The magnificent terminus of the East Coast Main Line hosted *Duchess of Sutherland* on 17 May 2010. Following arrival with the final leg of the Steam Dreams 'Coronation' charter, No 6233 is the centre of attention while simmering at the buffer stops. At the time, King's Cross was undergoing a major refurbishment programme, hence the sheeting over the roof. It had been opened by the Great Northern Railway in 1852, and is notable for the two arched train sheds together with a distinctive frontage and clock tower. However, it has more recently gained international recognition due to its connection with J. K. Rowling's 'Harry Potter' stories. *JW*

Right: **WELWYN VIADUCT**, or Digswell Viaduct, is located just south of Welwyn North station. Opened in 1850 by Queen Victoria, this massive 40-arch structure measures 1,560 feet in length and is 100 feet tall.

On 5 December 2015 a sharp westerly wind catches the exhaust of *Duchess of Sutherland* while heading the RTC's 'Lindum Fayre' from King's Cross to Lincoln. *JW*

Below right: **TEMPSFORD** is north of Sandy, and on 10 December 2016 *Duchess of Sutherland* carries suitably festive bunting while hauling a late-running RTC 'Christmas White Rose' from London King's Cross to York. *Paul Townsend*

Below: **OFFORD CLUNY** The pigeons roosting on the nearby ancient All Saints Church have been disturbed by the approach of a speeding *Duchess of Sutherland*, heading the final leg of the Steam Dreams 'Moors & Dales Express' from Scarborough to London Victoria on 18 September 2017. Note the diagonal yellow stripe on the cab-side sheet, which indicated a prohibition of working south of Crewe from 1 September 1964, due to the then energising of the overhead electric wires. Needless to say, it no longer applies! *JW*

The East Coast Main Line and connections

Below: **NEWARK-UPON-TRENT** The abandoned building, probably once a warehouse serving river traffic, is sandwiched between the River Trent and the ECML. On a grey and cold 21 December 2016 *Duchess of Sutherland* hurries through while heading the RTC 'Christmas White Rose' from Cambridge to York. *JW*

Above: **RETFORD** Later the same day *Duchess of Sutherland* passes through Retford station following a water stop with the returning 'Christmas White Rose' to Cambridge. The station lighting brings the whole scene to life, with No 46233 gently accelerating through the platform. *JW*

Above: **GAINSBOROUGH LEA ROAD** Originally set up under the joint control of the Great Northern and Great Eastern Railways, the GN&GE 'Joint Line', as it became known, nowadays connects Peterborough with Doncaster via Spalding, Sleaford, Lincoln and Gainsborough. It provides an effective relief and diversionary route to the ECML. On 18 September 2017 *Duchess of Sutherland* was routed over this line, while working the Steam Dreams 'Moors & Dales Express'. Gainsborough Lea Road station is situated at the end of a tight curve leading from Trent West and East Junctions, which are separated by the river of that name. East Junction is where the lines to Barnetby via Gainsborough Central station, and to Lincoln diverge. *Duchess of Sutherland* is taking the Lincoln line and is seen approaching Lea Road station. *JW*

Right: **SPALDING** was famous for its annual flower parade, an event that ran from 1959 to 2012. At the time much of the land surrounding the town was given over to the cultivation of tulips, which were the feature of the parade. The railway station remains an impressive structure, and is Grade II listed, although now only offers basic facilities. The charter train headed by *Duchess of Sutherland,* seen earlier at Gainsborough Lea Road, brings an element of variety from the usual diet of DMUs and freight workings passing through. *JW*

The East Coast Main Line and connections

DONCASTER was the birthplace of so many of Sir Nigel Gresley's iconic locomotives, probably the most famous being the streamlined Class 'A4s'. Sir William A Stanier's 'Princess Coronation' Class was the LMS response, and both of these classes were exceptionally fine locomotives and worthy of the esteem in which they are now held. It is always a poignant occasion when one passes through the birthplace of the other, as it was on 4 May 2014 with *Duchess of Sutherland* working through the centre road at Doncaster with the final leg of the RTC 'Great Britain VII' tour from York to King's Cross. *JW*

Right: **YORK** station is a magnificent edifice, as befits the 'railway town' founded by the legendary George Hudson, known as 'The Railway King'. He ensured that York became an important junction on the ECML, which it remains today. There is no finer sight than that of a steam-hauled train passing beneath the superb arched roof of the station, such as this working on 13 September 2003, with *Duchess of Sutherland* leading the PMR Tours 'Yorkshire Coast Coronation' from Leicester to Scarborough. *JW*

Below: **KNARESBOROUGH** Viaduct carries the line from York to Harrogate high above the River Nidd. The tower and petite steeple of the church of St John the Baptist is on the right, emerging from the treeline, as *Duchess of Sutherland* heads across the viaduct with a West Coast Railway 'Scarborough Spa Express' on 31 July 2007. *JW*

The East Coast Main Line and connections

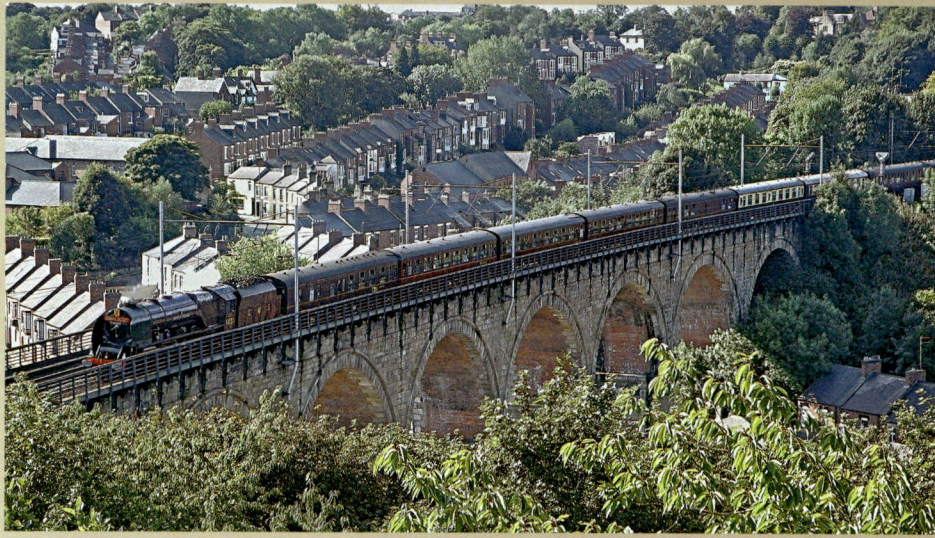

NEWCASTLE-UPON-TYNE The city and station are seen from the keep of the 12th-century castle as *Duchess of Sutherland* heads for Heaton Depot with the empty stock of the PMR Tours 'The North Eastern' from Sheffield on 17 October 2015, and is about to pass an incoming Northern Rail service formed of a Class 156 'Super Sprinter' DMU. *JW*

Above: **DURHAM VIADUCT** is seen from Wharton Park, which overlooks the city, the station and the viaduct. *Duchess of Sutherland* is seen passing high above Durham's rooftops on 8 September 2007 while hauling RTC's 'The Hadrian', a circular working from York via the Tyne Valley and Settle & Carlisle lines. *JW*

Right: **NEWCASTLE-UPON-TYNE** On a sunny 19 April 2014 *Duchess of Sutherland* awaits departure for Leicester with the returning PMR Tours 'North Eastern'. The graceful arches of the station's roof form a backdrop. *JW*

Right: **HEXHAM**, on the Tyne Valley line between Newcastle and Carlisle, boasts a distinctive elevated signal box that spans the running lines. On 8 September 2007 *Duchess of Sutherland* passes with 'The Hadrian' rail tour, seen on the previous page at Durham. The signal box is now just one of two such examples remaining. *JW*

Below: **SCARBOROUGH**, the premier East Coast resort, has been a regular destination for *Duchess of Sutherland* over the years. This is an early visit, on 11 May 2002, with the PMR Tours 'Scarborough Coronation' from Leicester, passing Falsgrave signal box and the landmark signal gantry. The signal box closed in 2010, and the gantry was donated to the North Yorkshire Moors Railway where, following a reduction in width, it was erected at the Whitby end of Grosmont station. *JW*

Right: **KITTYBREWSTER VIADUCT**, alternatively the Black or Bedlington Viaduct, is a well-known structure spanning the River Blyth in Northumberland on the 'Blyth & Tyne' network. Although freight-only, the lines do see some charter trains, such as the visit of *Duchess of Sutherland* on 1 October 2005, seen crossing the viaduct while heading the RTC 'Hadrian' charter from Doncaster to Morpeth. Plans are being formulated to restore passenger services over part of the line by 2024 *Bob Andrews*

The Midland Main Line

LONDON ST PANCRAS The magnificent southern terminus of the Midland Main Line is also now the UK terminus of the Eurostar network. These scenes date from before the massive reconstruction of the station for the introduction of international services, which resulted in it being renamed St Pancras International from 2007. It is a cold winter evening on 8 December 2001 as *Duchess of Sutherland* simmers at the buffer stops beneath the famous overall roof, having just arrived with Past Time Rail's 'Midlander' charter from Derby. Nowadays this part of the station is exclusively allocated to international services, so these are never-to-be-repeated images. This is thought to be the first ever visit of a 'Duchess' to St Pancras. *Both John F. Stiles*

Right: **WELLINGBOROUGH** station has a mixture of old and new, with a rebuilt footbridge not exactly in tune with the older station buildings. On 19 December 2015 *Duchess of Sutherland* sweeps around the tight curve through the station heading the RTC 'York Yuletide Express' from London Victoria to York. *JW*

Below: **SOULDROP** is roughly the mid-way point on the 4-mile climb from Sharnbrook to Sharnbrook Summit, where the gradient is an unrelenting 1 in 119 throughout. On 17 November 2018 *Duchess of Sutherland* has that climb well in hand while heading for York with another RTC 'York Yuletide Express', this time from Ealing Broadway. Note on the left that work has commenced to reinstate the fourth track as part of the electrification of the line.. *JW*

Above: **LANGHAM JUNCTION** signal box and level crossing is located a couple of miles north of Oakham on the line from Kettering, via Corby and Melton Mowbray, that rejoins the Midland Main Line at Syston Junction. *Duchess of Sutherland* is seen passing by with the 'York Yuletide Express' seen earlier at Wellingborough *(page 68)*. JW

Right: **BARROW-UPON-SOAR** *Duchess of Sutherland* heads for York on the down slow line with the RTC 'York Yuletide Express' from Ealing Broadway, previously seen at Souldrop (page 68). The original station at Barrow-upon-Soar, which closed in 1968, was positioned on the fast lines to the right, while the new station, opened in 1994, is located just beyond the second bridge in the background on the slow lines. JW

EAST MIDLANDS PARKWAY station, located in the shadow of Ratcliffe-on-Soar Power Station, opened in January 2009. It has good transport connections, with Junction 24 of the M1 motorway and East Midlands Airport both just a short distance away. The power station was commissioned in 1968 and is now one of the few remaining active coal-fired generators in the UK, and is scheduled to be the last to be closed in 2024. On 5 April 2017 *Duchess of Sutherland* passes by heading a Steam Dreams charter from Barrow Hill Locomotive Inspection Point (LIP) to London King's Cross. *JW*

The Midland Main Line

BELPER Here the Midland Main Line from Derby runs through a lined cutting that essentially bisects the town. *Duchess of Sutherland* is seen accelerating through the cutting on the approach to the station while heading the Vintage Trains 'Scarborough Flyer' from Tyseley on 29 June 2013. JW

ILKESTON is located on the Erewash Valley line, which offers a more direct route to Chesterfield by avoiding Derby. On 14 June 2014 *Duchess of Sutherland* approaches the town heading the PMR Tours 'Yorkshire Coronation' from Lincoln to Scarborough. The large mill bordering the line is no doubt connected to the lace industry, for which the town was famous. JW

DERBY station is seen on 6 May 2006 from the A6 bridge that spans the station throat. *Duchess of Sutherland* is departing at the head of the PMR Tours 'The Yorkshire Coronation' to Scarborough, which had earlier arrived diesel-hauled from Sheffield. The station has since been the subject of a major renovation and remodelling scheme. JW

CHESTERFIELD's defining landmark is the twisted spire of the Church of St Mary and All Saints, which is prominent on the right of this scene. On 19 October 2019 *Duchess of Sutherland* is seen breezing through the station at the head of the RTC 'Yorkshireman' from Ealing Broadway to York. JW

The Midland Main Line

NOTTINGHAM *Duchess of Sutherland* makes a spirited departure at the head of the PMR Tours 'London Explorer' from Derby to London King's Cross, via Grantham, on 6 October 2007. Staff at the DMU Stabling Point have turned out for the occasion. The building on the right with the gabled roof is the former goods shed. *JW*

NETHERFIELD JUNCTION is where the line east from Nottingham splits into separate routes for Lincoln and Grantham. On 17 October 2009 *Duchess of Sutherland* is heading for London King's Cross via Grantham and is seen passing Netherfield Junction signal box with the PMR Tours 'London Explorer' from Sheffield. *JW*

TOTON Traction Maintenance Depot is one of the largest such facilities in the UK, and is operated by DB Cargo, formerly known as EWS and later DB Schenker. Examples of Classes 08, 60, 66 and 67 can be seen lined up in front of the depot, all receiving the full force of the volcanic exhaust from *Duchess of Sutherland*, which is heading the RTC 'Yorkshireman' charter from Mill Hill to York on 22 March 2008. Ratcliffe-on-Soar Power Station can be seen on the horizon. *JW*

South and South West England

Above: **WHITCHURCH (Hants)** *Duchess of Sutherland* heads the return 'Cathedrals Express' from Yeovil Junction on 23 September 2017. The station is typified by the half-barrel roof on the up platform, and the solid station building. With lifting safety valves there is no need to push the locomotive as it is all downhill from here to Basingstoke. *JW*

Right: **WINCHFIELD** station is just beyond the far bridges as *Duchess of Sutherland* roars along the former London & South Western Railway's West of England main line heading a Steam Dreams London Victoria-Yeovil Junction working on 17 December 2019. *Ken Brunt*

Below: **ST MARY BOURNE VIADUCT**, or Hurstbourne Priors Viaduct, is located between Whitchurch (Hants) and Andover. On 23 September 2017 *Duchess of Sutherland* is seen traversing the viaduct while heading a Steam Dreams 'Cathedrals Express' from Faversham to Salisbury. *JW*

Right: **CHIPPING SODBURY TUNNEL** runs for 2½ miles beneath the Cotswold Hills between Badminton and Chipping Sodbury itself. On 17 June 2017 *Duchess of Sutherland* emerges from the western portal of the tunnel while heading the Vintage Trains 'Whispering Ghost' seen earlier at Leamington Spa *(page 44). JW*

Above: **WOKINGHAM** With the spire of St Paul's Parish Church visible in the background as *Duchess of Sutherland* heads for London Victoria, via Guildford and Redhill, with a returning Steam Dreams 'Cathedrals Express' from Oxford on 30 July 2008. *Ken Brunt*

Right: **CROFTON** Near Bedwyn, on the former GWR Berks & Hants Line, with *Duchess of Sutherland* speeding through the rain alongside the Kennet & Avon Canal while heading the RTC 'West Somerset Steam Express' from London Paddington to Minehead on 27 July 2019. *JW*

South and South West England

Right: **BRISTOL TEMPLE MEADS** On 27 October 2001 *Duchess of Sutherland* makes a spectacular departure at the head of Past Time Rail's 'The Mayflower' for Plymouth. This was to be the first of a number of workings for the 'Duchess' into Devon and Cornwall over subsequent years. *John F. Stiles*

Below: **COGLOAD JUNCTION** is just north of Taunton, where the lines from Bristol and London Paddington via Westbury meet, the former by way of a flyover to ease congestion. On 17 August 2019 *Duchess of Sutherland* has just passed beneath the Bristol line while heading the RTC 'West Somerset Steam Express' from London Paddington to Minehead. *JW*

Below right: **HUNTSPILL** is an artificial river crossing the Somerset Levels between Highbridge and Bridgwater, created in 1940 to provide high volumes of water to a newly created munitions factory. On 27 October 2001 *Duchess of Sutherland* is reflected in the Huntspill while heading 'The Mayflower' charter, seen above departing from Temple Meads. *JW*

Locomotives and Recollections: No 6233 *Duchess of Sutherland*

Left: **TEIGNMOUTH**
This elevated view is looking along the shore line towards Parson's Tunnel, with the coastline of East Devon beyond. The appearance of *Duchess of Sutherland* has generated crowds of onlookers as she heads the RTC 'Royal Duchy' to Par on 1 September 2019. *JW*

Right: **DAWLISH** Here along the sea wall the railway and the ocean often come into close contact, and conflict! The wall at this point is now subject to significant strengthening work to withstand future gales. This view of *Duchess of Sutherland*, on 28 August 2017, illustrates exactly how close the railway is to the sea. The train is an RTC 'Royal Duchy' working from Bristol to Par. *JW*

Right: **TEIGNMOUTH**
Duchess of Sutherland, working Past Time Rail's 'The Mayflower', has just emerged from Parson's Tunnel on 27 October 2001, one of five short tunnels that thread the railway around the exposed headland from Dawlish.
John F. Stiles

The South and South West England

Lefte: **PLYMOUTH NORTH ROAD** With the brute force of *Duchess of Sutherland* evidenced by the volcanic exhaust and furiously lifting safety valves, the driver cautiously eases the returning RTC 'Royal Duchy' from the station on 28 August 2017. *JW*

Below: **LARGIN VIADUCT** is one of several such structures that carry the Cornish main line along the Fowey Valley between Liskeard and Bodmin Road. On 1 September 2019 *Duchess of Sutherland* is seen crossing Largin viaduct on the difficult climb from Bodmin Road to Doublebois while heading the returning RTC 'Royal Duchy'. *JW*

Above: **ROYAL ALBERT BRIDGE, SALTASH** This was the view from the footplate of *Duchess of Sutherland* on 7 August 2016, while heading out of Cornwall onto Brunel's famous bridge. The train is a returning RTC 'Royal Duchy' from Par to Bristol. *Paul Wood*

COCKWOOD HARBOUR On 1 September 2019, at the end of a perfect day, just after sunset with the tide on the turn, *Duchess of Sutherland* is reflected in the waters of this small tidal inlet near Powderham while hurrying over the causeway with the returning RTC 'Royal Duchy', seen on the previous page at Largin. *JW*